# The Emancipation Proclamation

## by Ann Heinrichs

Content Adviser: Tim Townsend,
Historian, Lincoln Home National Historic Site,
Springfield, Illinois

Social Studies Adviser: Professor Sherry L. Field,
Department of Curriculum and Instruction, College of Education,
The University of Texas at Austin

Reading Adviser: Dr. Linda D. Labbo,
Department of Reading Education, College of Education,
The University of Georgia

## COMPASS POINT BOOKS

Minneapolis, Minnesota

Compass Point Books
3722 West 50th Street, #115
Minneapolis, MN 55410

Visit Compass Point Books on the Internet at *www.compasspointbooks.com* or e-mail your request to *custserv@compasspointbooks.com*


Photographs ©: Library of Congress, cover, 25, 30, 31, 32, 37; Stock Montage, 4, 5, 19, 28, 35; North Wind Picture Archives, 8, 10, 18, 21, 23, 24, 27; Hulton Getty/Archive Photos, 9, 11, 12, 15, 17, 36, 39, 40; Ohio Historical Society, 29.


Editors: E. Russell Primm, Emily J. Dolbear, and Deborah Cannarella
Photo Researchers: Svetlana Zhurkina and Jo Miller
Photo Selector: Linda S. Koutris
Designer: Bradfordesign, Inc.


**Library of Congress Cataloging-in-Publication Data**

Heinrichs, Ann.
    The Emancipation Proclamation / by Ann Heinrichs.
      p. cm. — (We the people)
    Includes bibliographical references and index.
    Summary: Looks at the political and moral issues that caused President Lincoln to issue the 1863 document that freed many slaves, and at the immediate and long-term consequences of his action.
    ISBN 0-7565-0209-8 (hardcover)
    1. United States. President (1861–1865 : Lincoln). Emancipation Proclamation—Juvenile literature.  2. Lincoln, Abraham, 1809–1865—Juvenile literature.  3. Slaves—Emancipation—United States—Juvenile literature.  4. United States—Politics and government—1861–1865—Juvenile literature. [1. Emancipation Proclamation. 2. Lincoln, Abraham, 1809–1865. 3. Slavery—History. 4. United States—History—Civil War, 1861–1865. 5. African Americans—History.] I. Title. II. We the people (Compass Point Books)
    E453 .H45 2002
    973.7'14—dc21                                                2001004739

# TABLE OF CONTENTS

# A DREAM OF FREEDOM

President Abraham Lincoln issued the Emancipation **Proclamation** on New Year's Day, 1863. In this important **document**, he said, "I do order and declare that all persons held as slaves . . . are, and henceforward shall be, free."

These powerful words were a dream come true for the 4 million slaves in the Southern United States. The Emancipation Proclamation didn't free all the nation's slaves, but it was a powerful promise of changes to come.

Lincoln had many reasons for issuing the Emancipation Proclamation. In 1863, the Civil War had already been going on for almost two years. Eleven Southern states had

*Abraham Lincoln*

4

seceded, or pulled away, from the Union. They had formed their own nation, called the Confederate States of America. Soldiers of the Confederate States of America were fighting the soldiers of the United States of America.

Lincoln wanted this war to end. He wanted to unite the country again. He wanted to rid the country of slavery.

*The Battle of Corinth took place during the Civil War.*

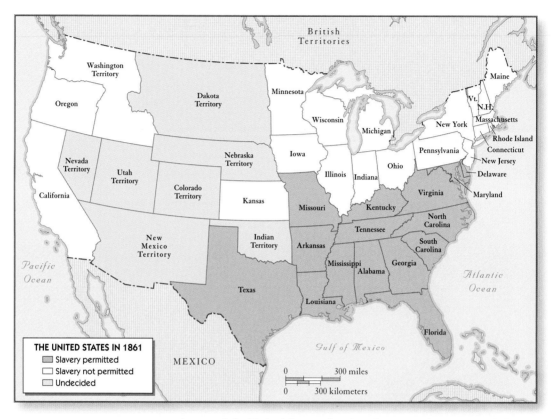

*A map of the United States showing the states that permitted slavery as well as those that prohibited it*

Lincoln had tried to end slavery for years, but the country was not ready for such a great change. Slaves had been bought and sold in America for more than 200 years. Congress and the American people were deeply divided about the issue of slavery. They could not agree about what to do.

Now, because the nation was at war, the president could make his own decision. He did not have to ask Congress to approve it. Lincoln used his power as president to help end the war and free the slaves in the South.

Many American people criticized Lincoln for his actions. Even people who were against slavery were unhappy about the proclamation. The slaves were not unhappy, though. Now they could see a clear road to freedom ahead of them. They knew that their dream was about to come true. They knew that it was only a matter of time before they were all "free at last."

# THE LONG ROAD

The Emancipation Proclamation was just one step on the long road to freedom. Long before the Civil War began, Northern states had outlawed slavery. In the Southern states, however, conditions were different. Huge plantations there grew row upon row of cotton and

*A plantation owner's home in Georgia*

tobacco. Many workers were needed to harvest the cotton. Plantation owners bought African slaves, many of whom were taken by force from their homelands to work in the fields.

*Slave families were often separated and sold to different owners.*

By the 1860s, 4 million slaves were working on Southern plantations. The labor was back- breaking, and the living conditions were dreadful. Many slave owners beat their slaves. They bought and sold them in the markets. Mothers and children, husbands and wives often were sold separately and never saw each other again.

Some slaves ran away, risking their lives to escape to freedom in the North. Many people helped these runaway slaves. These people were the **abolitionists**. They wanted to abolish, or get rid of, slavery. People of all races, social classes, and religions worked together against slavery.

*Frederick Douglass*

Frederick Douglass was one of the greatest abolitionists. This brilliant African-American man had escaped from slavery himself. As a freeman in the North, he became a writer and a powerful public speaker. He started an anti-slavery newspaper called the *North Star*. Later, he worked with President Abraham Lincoln.

Like many abolitionists, Douglass supported the Underground Railroad. This railroad was not the usual sort of railroad. It did not have a train. The Underground Railroad was a secret network of people who helped runaway slaves on their journey to freedom. In the dark of night, they hid runaway slaves in wagons, boats, and secret rooms.

The most famous "conductor" on the Underground Railroad was Harriet Tubman. After escaping from slavery herself, she led more than 300 slaves to safety and freedom in the North.

The Northern and Southern states could not agree about slavery. Members of the U.S. Congress argued about it, too.

In 1850, Congress passed the

*Harriet Tubman*

*This painting shows people escaping slavery on the Underground Railroad.*

Fugitive Slave Act. This law imposed heavy penalties on anyone who helped a runaway slave. It also allowed slave owners to hunt for their runaway slaves in the Northern states. After this law was passed, slaves had to travel all the way to Canada to be safe.

12

Congress also argued about the territories in the American West. Many territories wanted to become U.S. states. Some of them wanted to be Free States. Others—such as the territory of Missouri—wanted to be slave states. The congressmen could not agree and began making deals and **compromises**. In 1820, Congress passed the Missouri Compromise, which allowed Missouri to join the Union as a slave state. That same year, Maine joined the United States as a Free State. California joined as a Free State in 1850—the year in which the Fugitive Slave Act was passed.

These "deals" did not stop tempers from rising, however. The Southern states decided to secede from the United States. They declared themselves the Confederate States of America and chose Jefferson Davis as their president.

In April 1861, Confederate soldiers fired on Union troops in South Carolina. With those shots, the American Civil War began.

# A HOUSE DIVIDED

Lincoln had once warned the nation, "A house divided against itself cannot stand." Now, with America torn apart, the president was worried. The young country was not yet 100 years old. So many people had given their lives for freedom in the Revolutionary War (1775–1783). The American colonists had disagreements, but they had joined together to form a union of states. Would this new war mark the end of that union? Would the "house" come crashing down? Lincoln was deeply opposed to slavery, but his number one concern was the unity of the states.

In the early days of the war, the Confederates won some important battles against the Union soldiers. On September 17, 1862, however, Union forces won the Battle of Antietam in Maryland. The Confederacy felt the harsh blow, and President Lincoln took action quickly. He decided to issue a proclamation that would force the Southern states to end the war.

At that time, Lincoln did not have to ask Congress to approve his actions. The president of the United States is also the commander in chief. During wartime, the president is able to act on his own for the good of the nation.

*The Battle of Antietam*

# NEW YEAR'S DAY

On September 22, 1862, Lincoln issued the preliminary proclamation. This document was a warning to the Confederate States. Lincoln told them that if they were still fighting the Civil War on January 1, 1863, they would lose their slaves.

People throughout the country took notice. Half of them were afraid that Lincoln would not keep that promise. The other half were afraid that he would. The Confederate States did not stop fighting—and Lincoln kept his promise.

For the next 100 days, President Lincoln carefully worked on the words of the Emancipation Proclamation. By New Year's Eve, he was finally satisfied. The document was just the way he wanted it.

New Year's Day, 1863, was a busy day for the president. He rose early and thought about the many duties he had to perform that day. His first task excited him most. That morning, Secretary of State William H. Seward

*President Lincoln at work writing the proclamation*

arrived at the White House. Under his arm, Seward carried the document that Lincoln had worked on for so long. All the president had to do now was sign it.

William H. Seward

Lincoln carefully read the proclamation one last time to make sure that everything was perfect. But it was not! A clerk had added another line. Above the spot for Lincoln's signature, the clerk had written "I have . . . set my name." Lincoln did not like the phrase. He changed it to read "I have . . . set my hand." That's how the president usually ended his documents. It was not an important change, but Lincoln wanted every word to be just right. Seward sighed. He would have

18

to come back later to have the president sign the corrected document.

In the meantime, Lincoln had another job to do. He had to attend the annual New Year's Day **reception** at the White House. After chatting with many people and shaking hundreds of hands, the president was tired. But the day's most important event was yet to come.

*The first reading of the Emancipation Proclamation*

After the reception, Lincoln went upstairs to his study. There, on his desk, lay the five handwritten pages he had worked so hard to write. Lincoln checked to make sure that the clerk had changed the word as he had asked.

Just before he signed the proclamation, the president said, "I never in my life felt more certain that I was doing right than I do in signing this paper." Lincoln's proclamation freed many slaves. But slavery did not fully end until the Thirteenth **Amendment** to the Constitution was approved in 1865.

That night, a **telegraph** operator tapped out each word of the proclamation to newspapers far and wide. Lincoln strolled over to the telegraph station to watch the young man at work. Then Lincoln sank into a comfortable chair and put his feet up on the desk. It was the end of a very long and satisfying day.

*A busy American Telegraph Company office*

## CELEBRATION!

As news of the proclamation spread, celebrations broke out across the country. In the North, African-American preachers read the proclamation from their pulpits. In the South, Union soldiers gathered groups of slaves to read the words to them. The freed people cheered. Crowds of former slaves poured into the streets and celebrated throughout the night. Many white people celebrated, too. New Year's Day, 1863, was a day that no one would ever forget.

Most former slaves shouted with joy when they heard that they were free. Others were stunned. They had never known freedom. They wondered what it would be like to be free.

Many freedmen made plans to join the Union army. Other former slaves began packing to move out of the South. For them, anywhere away from the plantation would be fine! The former slave owners could not stop them now.

*African-Americans attending a church service*

Some freed slaves stayed on the plantations, however. They may not have been treated badly by their owners. Freedom was new to them, and they were not in a hurry to face the unknown changes and challenges.

Strange as it seems, many slaves did not know that they had been freed. Union soldiers had not yet reached them with

23

*Freed slaves leaving the plantation*

the news, and their masters would not tell them, of course. Some slaves in Texas did not hear that they were free until two years later!

On June 19, 1865, General Gordon Granger of the Union army read the Emancipation Proclamation in Galveston, Texas. The freed slaves celebrated the nine-

teenth of June as "June-
teenth." Each year after
that, they celebrated
Juneteenth with
church services, pic-
nics, barbecues, and
parades.

The Texas cele-
bration soon spread to
neighboring states. In
time, African-Americans
throughout the country
caught the spirit of

*General Gordon Granger*

Juneteenth. Even today, many people throughout America
celebrate Juneteenth as a festival of freedom.

# A POWERFUL MESSAGE

The Emancipation Proclamation did not instantly free all the slaves in the country. It freed the slaves only in those Southern states that were fighting against the Union.

Slavery was still legal in the border states that were loyal to the Union—Missouri, Kentucky, Maryland, and Delaware. Slavery also continued to exist in the Confederate areas controlled by the Union—Tennessee, West Virginia, and parts of Louisiana and Virginia.

Many abolitionists in the North were disappointed. They felt that Lincoln was just freeing slaves to weaken the South and win the war. They believed that too many people in America were still trapped in slavery. They also knew that the proclamation would have no meaning if the Union lost the war.

The proclamation did have great meaning, however. It changed the goals of the Civil War. After the proclamation was issued, the Civil War was no longer a war to save

*African-Americans celebrate the news of the Emancipation Proclamation*

the Union. It became a war for freedom, too. The proclamation sent a clear message to all Americans that slavery was no longer acceptable in a free country.

The proclamation changed the way the war was going, too. Freed slaves could now join the Union Army. Throughout the South, African-American men eagerly joined the fight for freedom. The numbers and strength of the Union army swelled accordingly.

These soldiers, once slaves themselves, now played an active part in ridding the country of slavery. With their help, their children would grow up free.

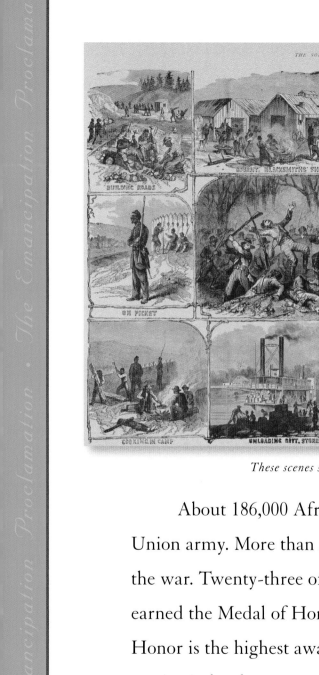

*These scenes show African-Americans as members of the Union army.*

About 186,000 African-American men joined the Union army. More than 37,000 of them lost their lives in the war. Twenty-three of these African-American soldiers earned the Medal of Honor for bravery. The Medal of Honor is the highest award a member of the military can receive in battle.

28

# "TILL I WAS FREE"

The Emancipation Proclamation changed the day-to-day lives of the freed slaves and gave hope to many others. In the 1930s, many former slaves talked to writers about their experiences. These simple stories bring to life the fight for freedom that was fought 150 years ago.

Richard Toler, for example, was born a slave on a plantation in Virginia. As a child, he tended cows and worked in the fields. When he was older, he became a blacksmith, making farm tools and horseshoes. After the Emancipation Proclamation, Richard wanted to be a Union soldier. He was not accepted into the army, however, because his health was poor.

*Richard Toler at about 100 years old*

29

After the Civil War, Richard moved to Ohio. For the next thirty-six years, he worked as a blacksmith. He went to night school and learned to read and write. He also taught himself to play the fiddle and was in great demand to play for dances. "I never had no good times till I was free," Richard said.

Mary Reynolds grew up as a slave in Louisiana. She and Sara, the master's daughter, often played together. One day, Union soldiers came onto the plantation. President Lincoln had just issued the Emancipation Proclamation. More than half the black men on the plantation left with the Union army. Mary and her mother had nowhere to go, so they stayed on the farm.

Soon, Mary's uncle in Texas sent them a letter. He would pay their way to come and live with him.

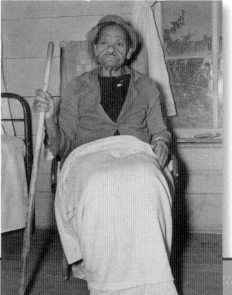

*Mary Reynolds at about 105 years old*

*Walter Calloway at 89 years old*

Mary married a man from Texas and got a job as a cook and housekeeper. Sara often wrote to Mary and asked her to visit her. Mary always hoped to see her old friend again, but she never returned to the plantation.

Walter Calloway was born in Virginia in 1848. When he was a baby, his master sold him, his mother, and his brother to a plantation owner in Alabama. At age ten, Walter was doing a man's job, plowing the fields. One day, Walter said, there was a big meeting in Montgomery, Alabama. "They elected Mister Jeff Davis president [of the Confederacy] and busted the United States wide open." Not long after that, "they told us we's free . . . and all the folks soon scattered all over."

Walter said that the freed slaves had to work just as hard as they did before they were free. Sometimes, he said,

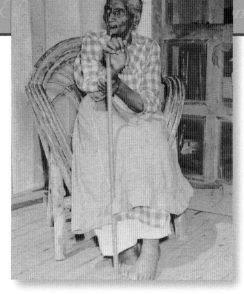

*Lucinda Davis at 89 years old*

they had even less than they did on the plantations. Still, Walter was happy that he was no longer a slave. He worked for the city of Birmingham, Alabama, until he retired.

Lucinda Davis never even knew her parents. When she was a child, Lucinda and her parents were sold to three different plantation owners in Oklahoma. All three masters were Creek Indians. Lucinda grew up speaking Creek. She took care of her owners' baby. Lucinda remembered eating roasted corn, deer meat, wild turkeys, and turtles. Her master cooked outdoors over a big fire.

After the Emancipation Proclamation, Lucinda's uncle went north to be a Union soldier, but Lucinda did not know she was free. She stayed with her master even after the Civil War. She was young and had nowhere else to go. One day, some men from the Creek Indian Agency found her. Her parents had been looking for her, and the family was united again. After she married, the government gave Lucinda and her husband land in Oklahoma to build a home.

Jourdon Anderson, his wife, and three children were slaves in Tennessee. By 1865, he and his family were free and moved to Ohio. Jourdon had a good job and a comfortable home. His children were going to school.

One day, he got a letter from his former master in Tennessee. The man invited Jourdon to come back to work for him and promised him good pay. Jourdon wrote back, asking for proof of good faith. He asked the former master to send him the wages he should have earned during his thirty-two years of service. Jourdon figured the amount was more than $11,000—a huge sum of money in those days. There is no record of the former master's reply to Jourdon's request.

# FARTHER ALONG THE ROAD

President Lincoln ran for reelection in 1864. During his **campaign,** he repeated one important message. He wanted to abolish slavery throughout the entire nation. The president won reelection, and Congress heard his message.

Early in 1865, President Lincoln sat at his desk and proudly signed the Thirteenth Amendment. This amendment to the U.S. Constitution abolished slavery in the United States. "This amendment is a king's cure for all the evils," Lincoln said. "It winds the whole thing up."

The Civil War ended on April 9, 1865. The Union victory was a great relief to President Lincoln. Finally, the country could join together again and move forward. Lincoln knew there was more work to do, however. Someday, he hoped to give former slaves the right to vote. Lincoln never had a chance to see all his dreams come true. Just five days after the Civil War ended, President

*The U.S. House of Representatives passing the Thirteenth Amendment*

Lincoln was shot and killed by an **assassin** named John Wilkes Booth.

In 1870, the Fifteenth Amendment was passed. This amendment gave men of all races the right to vote. African-American women—like all other American women—had to wait fifty more years, however, for the right to vote. In 1920, the Nine-teenth Amendment gave every woman in the United States the right to vote.

*John Wilkes Booth*

## "FREE AT LAST!"

For years after President Lincoln signed the Emancipation Proclamation, African-Americans celebrated that important event. They held parades with brass bands and marched to assembly halls to listen to readings of the Emancipation Proclamation. Important citizens gave speeches. Some called for equal rights. Others encouraged friendship and goodwill toward white people.

On the proclamation's fiftieth anniversary, African-American writer James Weldon Johnson wrote a memorial poem called "Fifty Years." It

*James Weldon Johnson*

37

was published on January 1, 1913. The poet urged all African-American people to take pride in the nation they helped to build:

> *This land is ours by right of birth,*
> *This land is ours by right of toil;*
> *We helped to turn its virgin earth,*
> *Our sweat is in its fruitful soil.*

In 1963, as the 100th anniversary of Lincoln's proclamation drew near, African-Americans prepared for the celebration. They had traveled far along the road to freedom—but they still had a long way to go.

At that time, African-Americans in the nation still did not have equal rights with whites. In many areas, they were not allowed to use the same restaurants, hotels, or movie theaters as white people. "White Only" and "Colored Only" signs hung near public drinking fountains and rest rooms. Some civil rights groups adopted the motto, "Free by '63."

38

One year later, Congress passed the Civil Rights Act of 1964. This law granted equal rights for all Americans in public places, public schools, and government programs. The Civil Rights Act was a great step forward—another step on the long road that the country has been traveling since before the Civil War.

*Before the Civil Rights Act was passed, blacks had to use separate rest rooms in public places.*

*Dr. Martin Luther King Jr. was an important leader in the civil rights movement.*

In 1963, civil rights leader Dr. Martin Luther King Jr. gave a famous speech in Washington, D.C. He reminded people of the Emancipation Proclamation and President Abraham Lincoln's promise.

"I have a dream," King said—"a dream of brotherhood for all." King spoke of a time when people of all races and religions would be free. When that time comes, he said, we can all join hands and sing: "Free at last! Free at last! Thank God Almighty, we are free at last!" People throughout the world still remember the words of Lincoln, King, and other great leaders—and still dream the same dream of freedom for all.

# GLOSSARY

abolitionists—people who fought to end slavery

amendment—a change made in a legal document

assassin—a person who kills an important person, such as a president

campaign—the speeches, visits, and other work done to win something, such as an election

compromises—solutions that settle differences between people

document—written or printed information

proclamation—an announcement

reception—a gathering held to welcome people

telegraph—a machine used to send messages in Morse code over wires

# DID YOU KNOW?

- During the Civil War, Harriet Tubman—a former slave—worked as a scout, a spy, and a nurse for the Union army.

- The Underground Railroad helped runaway slaves escape. It "ran" through fourteen Northern states into Canada. It also ran south to Mexico and the Caribbean.

- Cotton was such an important crop that some Southerners called it King Cotton.

# IMPORTANT DATES

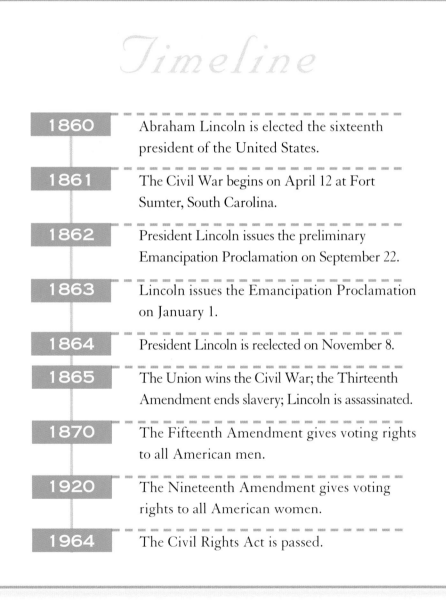

## Timeline

**1860**    Abraham Lincoln is elected the sixteenth president of the United States.

**1861**    The Civil War begins on April 12 at Fort Sumter, South Carolina.

**1862**    President Lincoln issues the preliminary Emancipation Proclamation on September 22.

**1863**    Lincoln issues the Emancipation Proclamation on January 1.

**1864**    President Lincoln is reelected on November 8.

**1865**    The Union wins the Civil War; the Thirteenth Amendment ends slavery; Lincoln is assassinated.

**1870**    The Fifteenth Amendment gives voting rights to all American men.

**1920**    The Nineteenth Amendment gives voting rights to all American women.

**1964**    The Civil Rights Act is passed.

# IMPORTANT PEOPLE

### FREDERICK DOUGLASS
**(1817–1895),** *former slave who became a leading abolitionist, writer, newspaper publisher, and public speaker*

### JAMES WELDON JOHNSON
**(1871–1938),** *African-American writer, statesman, and civil rights leader*

### DR. MARTIN LUTHER KING JR.
**(1929–1968),** *African-American minister and famous leader in the civil rights movement of the 1960s*

### ABRAHAM LINCOLN
**(1809–1865),** *sixteenth president of the United States who wrote the Emancipation Proclamation*

### HARRIET TUBMAN
**(1820–1913),** *former slave who became a leading abolitionist and the most famous "conductor" on the Underground Railroad*

# WANT TO KNOW MORE?

## At the Library

Branch, Muriel Miller. *Juneteenth: Freedom Day.* New York: Cobblehill/Dutton
   Books, 1998.

January, Brendan. *The Emancipation Proclamation.* Danbury, Conn.: Children's
   Press, 1997.

King, Wilma. *Children of the Emancipation.* Minneapolis: Carolrhoda Books, 2000.

Petry, Ann Lane. *Harriet Tubman: Conductor on the Underground Railroad.*
   New York: HarperTrophy, 1996.

Pinkney, Andrea Davis. *Abraham Lincoln: Letters from a Slave Girl.* Delray
   Beach, Fla.: Winslow Press, 2001.

## On the Web

**Emancipation Proclamation: Breaking the Bonds of Slavery**

*http://www.tbwt.com/interaction/lincoln/lincoln.htm*

For the document written by President Lincoln and more information about
slavery in America

**Excerpts from Slave Narratives**

*http://vi.uh.edu/pages/mintz/primary.htm*

For stories about the lives and experiences of freed slaves, told in their own words

## Through the Mail

**The National Archives**

National Archives and Records Administration

Archives 1 Research Support Branch (NWCC1)

Room 406

700 Pennsylvania Avenue, N.W.

Washington, DC 20408-0001

To get copies of the Emancipation Proclamation and other important documents

## On the Road

**The Lincoln Museum**

200 E. Berry Street

Fort Wayne, IN 46802

219/455-3864

To see exhibits, films, music, and multimedia computer activities about

Abraham Lincoln's life and family

# INDEX

**About the Author**

Ann Heinrichs was born in Fort Smith, Arkansas. She began playing the piano at age three and thought she would grow up to be a pianist. Instead, she became a writer. Now she has written more than fifty books for children and young adults. Ann Heinrichs lives in Chicago, Illinois.